Mastering 11+
English & Verbal Reasoning
Practice Book 1

ashkraft
EDUCATIONAL

Mastering 11+ © 2014 ashkraft educational

This page is intentionally left blank

Mastering 11+
English & Verbal Reasoning
Exercise Book 1

Copyright © 2014 ASHKRAFT EDUCATIONAL

ISBN: 1502481561
ISBN-13: 978-1502481566

DEDICATION

To all children preparing for the eleven plus exams and
the parents who want nothing but the best for their kids.

"Before anything else,

preparation is the key success"

Alexander Graham Bell

Table of Contents

MATCHING

WORDS

"One important key to success is self-confidence.
An important key to self-confidence is preparation"
Arthur Ashe

EXERCISE 1: Matching Words

Instructions: Select the word that has the same or closest meaning to the word on the left. There is only one correct answer for each question.

		A	B	C	D	E
1	SERENE	Bustling	Severe	Tranquil	Mist	Nature
2	LOATHE	Adore	Disdain	Worship	Love	Respect
3	ANTAGONIST	Friend	Foe	Guest	Politician	Alien
4	VERSATILE	Ingenious	Ugly	Inflexible	Stable	Immobile
5	VICIOUS	Kind	Humility	Meagre	Cruel	Caring
6	TORMENT	Agony	Cheer	Solace	Console	Soothe
7	TORRID	Cool	Serene	Calm	Stifling	Composed

8	FLASHY	A Flamboyant	B Understated	C Restrained	D Simple	E Light

9	FICKLE	A Unison	B Stable	C Harmony	D Humble	E Erratic

10	HUMILITY	A Modesty	B Flashy	C Vicious	D Flamboyant	E Stable

11	ASTUTE	A Stupid	B Simple	C Sharp	D Rash	E Foolish

12	CRINGE	A Recoil	B Handle	C Meet	D Face	E Encounter

13	BOUNTIFUL	A Fruitless	B Fruitful	C Bounty	D Scarce	E Limited

14	INCONSPICUOUS	A Distinct	B Indistinct	C Earthly	D Heavenly	E Obvious

15	NOVICE	A Apprentice	B Master	C Foolish	D Assistant	E Advice

Mastering 11+ ™ / English & VR – Book ONE / ashkraft educational

Instructions: Select the word that has the same or closest meaning to the word on the left. There is only one correct answer for each question.

		A	**B**	**C**	**D**	**E**
1	INVINCIBLE	Exposed	Helpless	Unbeatable	Weak	Susceptible
2	PRECEDING	Afterwards	Prior	Following	Subsequent	Resulting
3	CRAVEN	Spineless	Heroic	Daring	Sick	Brave
4	ABRUPT	Polite	Slow	Hasty	Civil	Gracious
5	ABSURD	Foolish	Lucid	Likely	Plausible	Sensible
6	VANISH	Motor	Disappear	Look	Seem	Vital
7	CONDEMN	Judge	Commend	Laud	Praise	Fight

8	SYNTHETIC	**A** ⊑ Artificial	**B** ⊑ Factual	**C** ⊑ Genuine	**D** ⊑ Authentic	**E** ⊑ Physical

9	SOFTEN	**A** ⊑ Relieve	**B** ⊑ Stimulate	**C** ⊑ Excite	**D** ⊑ Kindle	**E** ⊑ Inspire

10	RAMBLING	**A** ⊑ Confused	**B** ⊑ Concise	**C** ⊑ Succinct	**D** ⊑ Clear	**E** ⊑ Short

11	OVERTHROW	**A** ⊑ Long	**B** ⊑ Support	**C** ⊑ Uphold	**D** ⊑ Defend	**E** ⊑ Downfall

12	CERTAIN	**A** ⊑ Unsure	**B** ⊑ Deniable	**C** ⊑ Unclear	**D** ⊑ Evident	**E** ⊑ Hesitant

13	DEDICATED	**A** ⊑ Subdued	**B** ⊑ Apathetic	**C** ⊑ Steadfast	**D** ⊑ Casual	**E** ⊑ Unexcited

14	DUBIOUS	**A** ⊑ Certain	**B** ⊑ Suspicious	**C** ⊑ Assured	**D** ⊑ Clear	**E** ⊑ Evident

15	TIMID	**A** ⊑ Shy	**B** ⊑ Bold	**C** ⊑ Gallant	**D** ⊑ Brash	**E** ⊑ Impudent

Instructions: Select the word that has the same or closest meaning to the word on the left. There is only one correct answer for each question.

		A	B	C	D	E
1	HUMID	Dry	Waterless	Moist	Parched	Thirsty
2	PRESERVE	Crush	Overthrow	Demolish	Service	Conserve
3	DISCREET	Obvious	Subtle	Apparent	Actual	Evident
4	ABUNDANCE	Scarcity	Plenty	Shortage	Rarity	Dearth
5	PRECARIOUS	Safe	Hazardous	Innocuous	Harmless	Secure
6	OSCILLATE	Fixed	Unmoving	Fluctuate	Circle	Peripheral
7	FORTUNE	Prosperity	Poverty	Dearth	Scarcity	Lack

8	VARIABLE	A Constant	B Changeable	C Steady	D Uniform	E Consistent

9	PROVISIONAL	A Perpetual	B Constant	C Eternal	D Stable	E Interim

10	VOLATILE	A Fickle	B Predictable	C Stable	D Hot	E Capricorn

11	TANGIBLE	A Elusive	B Tangy	C Unknown	D Material	E Vague

12	ORIGINATE	A Original	B Instigate	C Complete	D Finale	E Polish

13	COMMITTED	A Casual	B Free	C Loyal	D Indifferent	E Tough

14	PROTEST	A Consent	B Campaign	C Confidence	D Approval	E Protect

15	SABOTAGE	A Hurt	B Repair	C Healing	D Overhaul	E Agitate

EXERCISE 4: Matching Words

Instructions: Select the word that has the same or closest meaning to the word on the left. There is only one correct answer for each question.

#	Word	A	B	C	D	E
1	FABRICATE	Destroy	Devise	Annihilate	Devastate	Demolish
2	IMPEDIMENT	Obstacle	Assistance	Structure	Treatment	Safety
3	PERILOUS	Unsafe	Secure	Harmless	Safe	Innocuous
4	BARRICADE	Facilitate	Assist	Accelerate	Expedite	Barrier
5	LONGWINDED	Boring	Music	Enlivening	Rousing	Energising
6	SCATTER	Distribute	Collect	Gather	Congregate	Cater
7	ANTHOLOGY	Compilation	Science	Medicine	Genre	Solitaire

8	ARBITRARY	A Systematic	B Logical	C Random	D Plausible	E Reasonable
9	SUCCINCT	A Rambling	B Pompous	C Talkative	D Boring	E Concise
10	VENEER	A Finish	B Begin	C Enemy	D Deer	E Far
11	SQUALID	A Filthy	B Neat	C Hygienic	D Sterile	E Fresh
12	AUTONOMOUS	A Independent	B Reliant	C Reliable	D Supported	E Unanimous
13	DELIBERATE	A Reflect	B Accidental	C Chance	D Unplanned	E Fortuitous
14	INTEGRITY	A Fraud	B Deceit	C Trickery	D Honesty	E Corrupt
15	WEARY	A Attire	B Vigorous	C Lively	D Careful	E Tired

Mastering 11+ ™ / English & VR – Book ONE / ashkraft educational

Instructions: Select the word that has the same or closest meaning to the word on the left. There is only one correct answer for each question.

1	DECEIVE	A ▭ Receive	B ▭ Accept	C ▭ Trustworthy	D ▭ Swindle	E ▭ Decision

2	COPIOUS	A ▭ Scant	B ▭ Duplicate	C ▭ Bearable	D ▭ Short	E ▭ Ample

3	ANXIETY	A ▭ Angst	B ▭ Calmness	C ▭ Reassurance	D ▭ Peace	E ▭ Composure

4	AMELIORATE	A ▭ Deteriorate	B ▭ Enhance	C ▭ Failure	D ▭ Depreciate	E ▭ Wane

5	BENEDICTION	A ▭ Approval	B ▭ Addiction	C ▭ Luxury	D ▭ Refusal	E ▭ Escape

6	INTREPID	A ▭ Fearless	B ▭ Devilish	C ▭ Behaviour	D ▭ Internal	E ▭ Integrity

7	LUMINOUS	A ▭ Radiant	B ▭ Cloudy	C ▭ Dismal	D ▭ Faded	E ▭ Dreary

8	BRAZEN	A Discreet	B Audacious	C Subtle	D Cautious	E Diplomatic
9	LESION	A Academic	B Fix	C Mend	D Cure	E Wound
10	SECURE	A Secret	B Release	C Acquire	D Reduce	E Spy
11	MESSY	A Unkempt	B Neat	C Miserable	D Abscond	E Plenty
12	BANAL	A Original	B Painful	C Bane	D Boring	E Native
13	TRAIT	A Feature	B Popular	C Deceive	D Manor	E Profession
14	GANDER	A Wander	B Peek	C Brave	D Meek	E Traveller
15	BEWILDER	A Confuse	B Clarify	C Wild	D Simplify	E Illuminate

Mastering 11+ ™ / English & VR – Book ONE / ashkraft educational

EXERCISE 6: Matching Words

Instructions: Select the word that has the same or closest meaning to the word on the left. There is only one correct answer for each question.

		A	B	C	D	E
1	TEPID	Enthusiastic	Lukewarm	Keen	Animated	Fervent
2	STROLL	Amble	Luxury	Bread	Dough	Sudden
3	ALOOF	Friendly	Detached	Open	Kindly	Gracious
4	GRATING	Annoying	Pleasant	Amusing	Lovely	Nice
5	INTERROGATE	Entrance	Probe	Arrogant	Rude	Lurid
6	MIGRATE	Drift	Headache	Pain	Refugee	Space
7	ACQUIRE	Lease	Procure	Stream	Evade	Mislay

8	BARE	A Tolerate	B Endure	C Simple	D Covered	E Roofed
9	DEFICIENT	A Defeatist	B Abundant	C Efficient	D Lacking	E Adequate
10	INDEPENDENT	A Reliant	B Autonomous	C Biased	D Supported	E Related
11	PARCHED	A Thrust	B Revived	C Charged	D Thirsty	E Restored
12	VULNERABLE	A Susceptible	B Invincible	C Impervious	D Supreme	E Unbeatable
13	EBB	A Subside	B Surge	C Wave	D Gush	E Pour
14	REFERENDUM	A Poll	B Sustain	C Oppose	D Reject	E Accept
15	SECRETION	A Secretive	B Discharge	C Discrete	D Absorb	E Enter

Instructions: Select the word that has the same or closest meaning to the word on the left. There is only one correct answer for each question.

		A	B	C	D	E
1	RECUPERATE	Render	Elude	Recover	Evade	Drop
2	ANNUL	Yearly	Cancel	Prolong	Valid	Disgust
3	ENCHANTED	Disgusted	Fascinated	Repelled	Appalled	Dismayed
4	EXORBITANT	Outrageous	Reasonable	Affordable	Intelligent	Rational
5	UTTERLY	Bitter	Hardly	Completely	Scarcely	Barely
6	COHERENT	Rational	Invalid	Irrational	Inconsistent	Togetherness
7	SOLILOQUY	Speech	Singer	Dancer	Athlete	Exaggerate

8	AUDACITY	A Stupidity	B Meek	C Cowardice	D Swagger	E Fear

9	ENDEMIC	A Restricted	B Widespread	C Regulated	D Limited	E Secretive

10	TROUGH	A Crib	B Ridge	C Edge	D Range	E Wrinkle

11	CHIDE	A Praise	B Exclaim	C Reprimand	D Honour	E Adore

12	BICKER	A Argue	B Agree	C Accept	D Cheat	E Deceive

13	FRIGID	A Torrid	B Freezing	C Stifling	D Baking	E Sizzling

14	REPELLENT	A Attractive	B Revolting	C Awaken	D Disgusting	E Proof

15	TEMPEST	A Blizzard	B Serene	C Calm	D Tranquillity	E Quiet

OPPOSITE WORDS

"The best preparation for good work tomorrow
is to do good work today"
Elbert Hubbard

EXERCISE 8: Opposite Words

Instructions: Select the word that has the opposite meaning to the word on the left. There is only one correct answer for each question.

1 **FACETIOUS**

A	B	C	D	E
Grave	Comical	Silly	Frivolous	Foolish

2 **LAVISH**

A	B	C	D	E
Extravagant	Thrifty	Swift	Lasting	Casual

3 **RATIONAL**

A	B	C	D	E
Logical	Abide	Partial	Confused	Idea

4 **PROMINENT**

A	B	C	D	E
Notable	Unknown	Famous	Failure	Inexperienced

5 **OUTLANDISH**

A	B	C	D	E
Strange	Unusual	Bizarre	Ordinary	Selfish

6 **OBSCURE**

A	B	C	D	E
Apparent	Obvious	Uncertain	Anxious	Hide

7 **GULLIBLE**

A	B	C	D	E
Discerning	Innocent	Credulous	Naïve	Trusting

8	FORMIDABLE	A Strong	B Powerful	C Insignificant	D Infirm	E Stable
9	INTENTIONAL	A Planned	B Purposely	C Accidental	D Deliberate	E Logical
10	UNPRODUCTIVE	A Efficient	B Inefficient	C Wasteful	D Improbable	E Unplanned
11	AMBIGOUS	A Approximate	B Vague	C Precise	D Detailed	E Defined
12	CURTAIL	A Length	B Shorten	C Elongate	D Shrink	E Dry
13	RAMBLING	A Concise	B Incoherent	C Tedious	D Confused	E Digressive
14	TACTFUL	A Diplomatic	B Considerate	C Subtle	D Forthright	E Skilfull
15	CONDEMN	A Absolve	B Sentence	C Judge	D Convict	E Reject

EXERCISE 9: Opposite Words

Instructions: Select the word that has the opposite meaning to the word on the left. There is only one correct answer for each question.

		A	B	C	D	E
1	SAGACIOUS	Wisdom	Judgment	Intelligent	Saintly	Foolish
2	DEDICATED	Staunch	Unfaithful	Keen	Steadfast	Loyal
3	MUFFLE	Silence	Deaden	Dampen	Amplify	Relieve
4	SCARCITY	Rarity	Dearth	Shortage	Paucity	Surplus
5	FRIVOLOUS	Dizzy	Playful	Funny	Joyous	Grim
6	HAPHAZARD	Chaotic	Systematic	Random	Jumbled	Messy
7	INCLEMENT	Pleasant	Severe	Foul	Windy	Squally

8	POMPOUS	A Modest	B Vain	C Arrogant	D Conceited	E Superior
9	PASSIVE	A Reflexive	B Lifeless	C Flaccid	D Active	E Reactive
10	ARTIFICIAL	A Imitation	B Fake	C Natural	D Organic	E Mock
11	QUIET	A Inaudible	B Discreet	C Soundless	D Raucous	E Pricking
12	TRANQUIL	A Soothing	B Calm	C Still	D Composed	E Noisy
13	CRAVEN	A Heroic	B Fearful	C Plead	D Spineless	E Cowardly
14	SUCCINCT	A Concise	B Crisp	C Longwinded	D Neat	E Brief
15	PERILOUS	A Extreme	B Risky	C Hazardous	D Unsafe	E Benign

EXERCISE 10: Opposite Words

Instructions: Select the word that has the opposite meaning to the word on the left. There is only one correct answer for each question.

#	Word	A	B	C	D	E
1	ABSURD	Observe	Farcical	Ludicrous	Strange	Sensible
2	UGLY	Beautiful	Horrible	Dreadful	Horrid	Nasty
3	FREQUENTLY	Recurrently	Seldom	Commonly	Often	Normally
4	FAMINE	Dearth	Scarcity	Plenty	Shortage	Starvation
5	STAGNATE	Idle	Decay	Fester	Progress	Bravery
6	SUBSTANTIATE	Validate	Disprove	Confirm	Verify	Substance
7	VENGEFUL	Unforgiving	Resentful	Charitable	Bitter	Ruthless

8	WISE	A Informed	B Elderly	C Aware	D Shrewd	E Irrational
9	SAFE	A Benign	B Harmless	C Secure	D Insecure	E Innocent
10	FEEBLE	A Frail	B Delicate	C Pathetic	D Poor	E Effective
11	IMPOVERISHED	A Bankrupt	B Destitute	C Indigent	D Important	E Enriched
12	STAGNANT	A Immobile	B Motionless	C Inactive	D Staggering	E Active
13	RESENTFUL	A Angry	B Bitter	C Offended	D Agree	E Insulted
14	BEDLAM	A Turmoil	B Mayhem	C Chaos	D Order	E Anarchy
15	CHUBBY	A Chunky	B Plump	C Stout	D Slim	E Heavy

EXERCISE 11: Opposite Words

Instructions: Select the word that has the opposite meaning to the word on the left. There is only one correct answer for each question.

1	EQUABLE	A ▭ Variable	B ▭ Unable	C ▭ Superior	D ▭ Calm	E ▭ Placid

2	TOLERATE	A ▭ Forbid	B ▭ Abide	C ▭ Stomach	D ▭ Allow	E ▭ Speed

3	EXCEPT	A ▭ Including	B ▭ Accept	C ▭ Excluding	D ▭ Bar	E ▭ But

4	TENANT	A ▭ Occupant	B ▭ Resident	C ▭ Landlord	D ▭ Renter	E ▭ Decimal

5	POTENT	A ▭ Strong	B ▭ Mighty	C ▭ Weak	D ▭ Convincing	E ▭ Forceful

6	FRET	A ▭ Worry	B ▭ Bother	C ▭ Upset	D ▭ Calm	E ▭ Agonise

7	DEARTH	A ▭ Surplus	B ▭ Lack	C ▭ Drought	D ▭ Famine	E ▭ Need

8	TRITE	A	B	C	D	E
		Tired	Banal	Original	Duplicate	Characteristic

9	BAFFLE	A	B	C	D	E
		Confuse	Puzzle	Clarify	Mystify	Stump

10	ARTICULATE	A	B	C	D	E
		Lucid	Clear	Eloquent	Mumble	Pronounce

11	GROW	A	B	C	D	E
		Nurture	Flourish	Sprout	Shrink	Escalate

12	PRETENTIOUS	A	B	C	D	E
		Modest	Conceited	Hallow	Pompous	Fake

13	WITHDRAWN	A	B	C	D	E
		Reserved	Introvert	Removed	Resigned	Extrovert

14	PETRIFY	A	B	C	D	E
		Alarm	Frighten	Scare	Panic	Comfort

15	FERVENT	A	B	C	D	E
		Fanatical	Intense	Keen	Vehement	Unresponsive

EXERCISE 12: Opposite Words

Instructions: Select the word that has the opposite meaning to the word on the left. There is only one correct answer for each question.

#	Word	A	B	C	D	E
1	WITTY	Clever	Funny	Entertaining	Sharp	Dismal
2	GENEROUS	Lavish	Plentiful	Meagre	Liberal	Kind
3	POTENT	Strong	Mighty	Weak	Convincing	Forceful
4	OBSTINATE	Stubborn	Adamant	Compliant	Persistent	Fixed
5	ADVERSE	Hostile	Bad	Positive	Negative	Unhelpful
6	INEPT	Competent	Clumsy	Hopeless	Bungling	Unskilled
7	DISTRAUGHT	Calm	Disturbed	Flustered	Worried	Distressed

8	ABROAD	A Home	B Overseas	C Aboard	D Away	E Island

9	CAPTIVE	A Caged	B Imprisoned	C Free	D Confined	E Enslaved

10	MALICIOUS	A Kind	B Nasty	C Cruel	D Evil	E Wicked

11	COLOSSAL	A Tiny	B Titanic	C Gigantic	D Immense	E Oversize

12	INVERSE	A Opposite	B Invert	C Reverse	D Introvert	E Identical

13	DISCRETION	A Preference	B Prudence	C Choice	D Indecision	E Foresight

14	INDISCREET	A Reckless	B Careful	C Imprudent	D Nosy	E Independent

15	EUPHORIC	A Blissful	B Overjoyed	C Despairing	D Excited	E Exultant

EXERCISE 13: Opposite Words

Instructions: Select the word that has the opposite meaning to the word on the left. There is only one correct answer for each question.

1	INDOLENT	A Lazy	B Sluggish	C Energetic	D Lethargic	E Idle

2	CAPACIOUS	A Cramped	B Spacious	C Ample	D Voluminous	E Vast

3	CONTEMPORARY	A Modern	B Current	C Old	D Recent	E Fresh

4	TREACHERY	A Loyalty	B Deceit	C Treason	D Betrayal	E Disloyalty

5	SOLITARY	A Sociable	B Individual	C Single	D Private	E Introverted

6	FIDDLE	A Swindle	B Hoax	C Ignore	D Cheat	E Manipulate

7	SCOUR	A Burnish	B Polish	C Dirty	D Wash	E Clean

8	**ABANDON**	**A** Reckless	**B** Leave	**C** Desert	**D** Restraint	**E** Wildness

9	**GENEROUS**	**A** Meagre	**B** Kind	**C** Liberal	**D** Charitable	**E** Plentiful

10	**FLOUNDER**	**A** Dither	**B** Delay	**C** Hesitate	**D** Slick	**E** Waver

11	**MAGNIFY**	**A** Enlarge	**B** Boost	**C** Shrink	**D** Magnetic	**E** Repellent

12	**INGENIOUS**	**A** Resourceful	**B** Cunning	**C** Original	**D** Ordinary	**E** Inspired

13	**REBUFF**	**A** Snub	**B** Decline	**C** Accept	**D** Repulse	**E** Spurn

14	**DEVOUR**	**A** Gobble	**B** Consume	**C** Engulf	**D** Conserve	**E** Destroy

15	**JUVENILE**	**A** Young	**B** Immature	**C** Mature	**D** Childish	**E** Youthful

EXERCISE 14: Opposite Words

Instructions: Select the word that has the opposite meaning to the word on the left. There is only one correct answer for each question.

1	**PIOUS**	A Irreverent	B Religious	C Spiritual	D Saintly	E Godly

2	**ENCRYPT**	A Decode	B Scramble	C Translate	D Encode	E Convert

3	**INEPT**	A Competent	B Clumsy	C Hopeless	D Bungling	E Unskilled

4	**ABBREVIATE**	A Truncate	B Condense	C Elongate	D Curtail	E Absorb

5	**WICKED**	A Villainous	B Criminal	C Respectable	D Depraved	E Unpleasant

6	**ARTFUL**	A Clever	B Open	C Sneaky	D Wily	E Crafty

7	**WOBBLE**	A Sway	B Quaver	C Dither	D Waver	E Steady

Mastering 11+ ™ / English & VR – Book ONE / ashkraft educational

8	WRETCHED	A Dejected	B Worthless	C Happy	D Spooky	E Energetic

9	RAGE	A Frenzy	B Craze	C Fad	D Ire	E Peace

10	EXALTED	A Illustrious	B Grand	C Lowly	D Lofty	E Dignified

11	GORY	A Pleasant	B Gruesome	C Ghastly	D Horrible	E Violent

12	AGONY	A Ecstasy	B Worry	C Misery	D Distress	E Aged

13	SAINTLY	A Righteous	B Evil	C Flawless	D Godly	E Pious

14	DEMOCRACY	A Equality	B Consensus	C inequality	D Fairness	E Republic

15	TORMENT	A Bane	B Delight	C Agony	D Anguish	E Annoyance

INCOMPLETE WORDS

"The best preparation for good work tomorrow
is to do good work today"
Elbert Hubbard

EXERCISE 15: Complete the word

Instructions: Complete the word on the right by filling the blank blocks, so that the word formed means the same, as the word on the left.

1	Smirk	G			N	

2	Content	H	A			Y

3	Dearth	L			K

4	Glum	M		R		S	E

5	Fray	F	R	A			S

6	Froth	F		A	

7	Fusion	B	L	E		

8	Gaudy	L			D		
9	Gawky	C	L	U	M		
10	Hector	H	A	S	S		
11	Hoot	H			K		
12	Kindle	S	P		R		
13	Illicit		L	L		G	A	L
14	Infuse	F			L		
15	Innate	N		T	I		E

Instructions: Complete the word on the right by filling the blank blocks, so that the word formed means the same, as the word on the left.

1	Sway	R	U		

2	Vouch	A	S	S	U		

3	Wither	F		D	

4	Meadow	F		E	L	

5	Meddle	I	N		A		E

6	Nomad	M	I		R	A	N	

7	Notion	I			A	

8	Oasis	R	E		U	G	

9	Altitude	H	E		G		T	

10	Hoax	P	R			K	

11	Snare	T			P	

12	Leap	H		K	

13	Hubbub	R	A	C			T	

14	Meek	M			D	

15	Sullen	M	O		O	S	

Instructions: Complete the word on the right by filling the blank blocks, so that the word formed means the same, as the word on the left.

1	Ramble	W		L	

2	Memoir	B	I		G	R		P	H	Y

3	Mellow	S	M	O			H

4	Docile	M			K

5	Meagre	P	A		T	R	

6	Forage	F	O		D	E	

7	Mirage	I	L		U	S	I		N

8	Mobile	M	O		A		L	E

9	Authentic	G	E		U		N	E

10	Taunt	I	N		U		T	

11	Titter	G	I			L	E	

12	Scowl	F	R		W		

13	Gore	V	I		L	E	N	C	

14	Snatch	S	E		Z		

15	Eerie	S	P			K	Y	

Mastering 11+ ™ / English & VR – Book ONE / ashkraft educational

EXERCISE 18: Complete the word

Instructions: Complete the word on the right by filling the blank blocks, so that the word formed means the same, as the word on the left.

1 Whine

W	H		N		E

2 Cascade

F	L			

3 Hinder

H	A		P		R

4 Waft

B	R		E	Z	

5 Mortar

C	E		E	N	

6 Swindle

F		A	U	

7 Stroll

W	A		

8	Rite	R	I		U	A	

9	Carton	C	O	N	T	I	N	E	

10	Shatter	D	E		T	R		Y

11	Wail	W	H		N	

12	Bale	B	U		D	L	

13	Muddled	C	H		O	T	I	

14	Pious	S	I		C	E	R	

15	Gory	G	H		S	T	L	

Mastering 11+ ™ / English & VR – Book ONE / ashkraft educational

EXERCISE 19: Complete the word

Instructions: Complete the word on the right by filling the blank blocks, so that the word formed means the same, as the word on the left.

1 Inform

A	D		I	S	

2 Mischief

M	A	L		C	

3 Charity

H	E		

4 Renew

R	E		A	I	

5 Abbreviate

S	H	O		T		N

6 Memoir

C	H	R	O	N	I		L

7 Ascent

R		S	

8	Solicitude	K		N	D	N	E		S

9	Brittle	F	R	A		I	L	

10	Gratuity	B	O	N		

11	Censure	S	C			N

12	Adorn	D	E		O		A	T	E

13	Ally	F	R	I			D

14	Forsake	Q		I	

15	Gallant	B	R		V	

Instructions: Complete the word on the right by filling the blank blocks, so that the word formed means the same, as the word on the left.

1	Husk	S	H	E		

2	Inferno	B	L	A		

3	Macabre	G	H	A			L	Y

4	Treachery	B	E	T	R		Y	A	

5	Visage	L	O			

6	Manacles	S	H	A	C	K		E	

7	Incline	S	L	O		

8	Horizon	P	R	O	S	p	E		

9	Grimace	S		I	R	

10	Sheaf	B	U	N	D	

11	Garret	A	T	T		

12	Bewilder	C	O	N		U		E

13	Saying	C	L	I	C		

14	Snooty	A	L	O		

15	Icicle	P	I	L		A	

Mastering 11+ ™ / English & VR – Book ONE / ashkraft educational

EXERCISE 21: Complete the word

Instructions: Complete the word on the right by filling the blank blocks, so that the word formed means the same, as the word on the left.

1 Wry

I	R		O		I	

2 Attorney

L			Y	E	R

3 Podium

P	L	A	T	F			M

4 Seizure

A	R		E		T

5 Landscape

S	C	E	N			Y

6 Impede

O	B	S	T			C	T

7 Fright

S	H	O		

8	Tranquility	C	A		

9	Savour	T	A	S		

10	Relegate	D	E	M			E

11	Segregate	S	E	P			A	T	E

12	Investigate	E	N				I	R	E

13	Wrath	A	N			R

14	Minimum	L	O			S	T

15	Velocity	S	P			D

ODD ONE OUT

"Success is where preparation meets opportunity"
Bobby Unser

EXERCISE 22: Odd word out

Instructions: Select the word from the each group of words that does not belong to that group.

1	A ☐ monk	B ☐ prince	C ☐ Ironmonger	D ☐ baroness	E ☐ priest

2	A ☐ Knife	B ☐ Lancet	C ☐ Cleaver	D ☐ Chauffeur	E ☐ Forceps

3	A ☐ Overthrow	B ☐ Coup	C ☐ Brave	D ☐ Conquer	E ☐ Downfall

4	A ☐ Annual	B ☐ Monthly	C ☐ Weekly	D ☐ Daily	E ☐ Century

5	A ☐ Prophecy	B ☐ Prediction	C ☐ Legacy	D ☐ Forecast	E ☐ Insight

6	A ☐ Avoid	B ☐ Elude	C ☐ Evade	D ☐ Avail	E ☐ Escape

7	A ☐ Quick	B ☐ Rapid	C ☐ Swift	D ☐ Hurry	E ☐ Instant

8	**A** Frisky	**B** Lamb	**C** Sober	**D** Swift	**E** Timid

9	**A** Vigil	**B** Inspect	**C** Guard	**D** Watch	**E** Celebrate

10	**A** Miles	**B** Metres	**C** Feet	**D** Kilometres	**E** Litre

11	**A** Tomato	**B** Orange	**C** Carrot	**D** Apple	**E** Grapes

12	**A** Grease	**B** Drill	**C** Hammer	**D** Spanner	**E** Pliers

13	**A** Catastrophe	**B** Ruin	**C** Disaster	**D** Calamity	**E** Mistrust

14	**A** Hawk	**B** Canary	**C** Crane	**D** Owl	**E** Herring

15	**A** Amsterdam	**B** India	**C** Malaysia	**D** France	**E** Mexico

EXERCISE 23: Odd word out

Instructions: Select the word from the each group of words that does not belong to that group.

	A	B	C	D	E
1	Apple	Clementine	Orange	Lemon	Grapefruit

	A	B	C	D	E
2	Obtain	Lean	Gain	Secure	Procure

	A	B	C	D	E
3	Eliminate	Abolish	Discharge	Engulf	Expel

	A	B	C	D	E
4	Durham	Sussex	York	Essex	Surrey

	A	B	C	D	E
5	Rare	Scarce	Unusual	Moderate	Extraordinary

	A	B	C	D	E
6	English	Hebrew	Scots	Welsh	Irish

	A	B	C	D	E
7	Run	Wicket	Pitch	Goal	Boundary

8	A Rubbish	B Trash	C Garbage	D Scratch	E Junk

9	A Erudite	B Learned	C Universal	D Scholarly	E Intellectual

10	A Gun	B Cashier	C Clown	D Cobbler	E Farmer

11	A Prompt	B Swift	C Hasty	D Quick	E Promote

12	A Disaster	B Catastrophe	C Ruin	D Misgiving	E Misfortune

13	A Pig	B Horse	C Leopard	D Sheep	E Goat

14	A Horrible	B Tranquil	C Awful	D Terrible	E Dreadful

15	A Spain	B Germany	C India	D Italy	E France

EXERCISE 24: Odd word out

Instructions: Select the word from the each group of words that does not belong to that group.

1	A ☐ Calf	B ☐ Cygnet	C ☐ Hob	D ☐ Cub	E ☐ Drake

2	A ☐ Plumber	B ☐ Nurse	C ☐ Mason	D ☐ Carpenter	E ☐ Miner

3	A ☐ Striker	B ☐ Back	C ☐ Forward	D ☐ Referee	E ☐ Goalkeeper

4	A ☐ Bale	B ☐ Batch	C ☐ Cluster	D ☐ Fleet	E ☐ Herring

5	A ☐ Permission	B ☐ Omission	C ☐ Consent	D ☐ Approval	E ☐ Clearance

6	A ☐ Produce	B ☐ Manufacture	C ☐ Make	D ☐ Consume	E ☐ Create

7	A ☐ Basket	B ☐ Purse	C ☐ Trunk	D ☐ Scabbard	E ☐ Kettle

8	A ▭ Stiff	B ▭ Rigid	C ▭ Firm	D ▭ Flexible	E ▭ Inelastic

9	A ▭ Plan	B ▭ Strategy	C ▭ Proposal	D ▭ Blueprint	E ▭ Bluesy

10	A ▭ Corn	B ▭ Cabbage	C ▭ Pork	D ▭ Peanut	E ▭ Peas

11	A ▭ Muster	B ▭ Nest	C ▭ Nide	D ▭ Pace	E ▭ Silk

12	A ▭ Pigeon	B ▭ Raven	C ▭ Flounder	D ▭ Partridge	E ▭ Pelican

13	A ▭ Azure	B ▭ Denim	C ▭ Sapphire	D ▭ Navy	E ▭ Pearl

14	A ▭ Nepal	B ▭ India	C ▭ Malaysia	D ▭ Mexico	E ▭ Sri Lanka

15	A ▭ Feta	B ▭ Cheddar	C ▭ Brie	D ▭ Cheese	E ▭ Mozzarella

EXERCISE 25: Odd word out

Instructions: Select the word from the each group of words that does not belong to that group.

1	A ☐ Bear	B ☐ Eagle	C ☐ Lamb	D ☐ Sheep	E ☐ Duck

2	A ☐ Overthrow	B ☐ Coup	C ☐ Brave	D ☐ Conquer	E ☐ Downfall

3	A ☐ Abbess	B ☐ Sultana	C ☐ Nanny	D ☐ Heroine	E ☐ Earl

4	A ☐ Legend	B ☐ Lore	C ☐ Festive	D ☐ Myth	E ☐ Tale

5	A ☐ Trivial	B ☐ Crucial	C ☐ Petty	D ☐ Minor	E ☐ Trifling

6	A ☐ Loch	B ☐ Torrent	C ☐ Trough	D ☐ Zenith	E ☐ Channel

7	A ☐ Fencing	B ☐ Football	C ☐ Tennis	D ☐ Hymns	E ☐ Yachting

Mastering 11+ ™ / English & VR – Book ONE / ashkraft educational

8	A ▭ Oak	B ▭ Tin	C ▭ Zinc	D ▭ Copper	E ▭ Gold

9	A ▭ Boy	B ▭ Girl	C ▭ Man	D ▭ Lad	E ▭ Chap

10	A ▭ Suspect	B ▭ Unsure	C ▭ Shady	D ▭ Fishy	E ▭ Suspense

11	A ▭ Amusement	B ▭ Glee	C ▭ Pleasure	D ▭ Magical	E ▭ Pastime

12	A ▭ Miserable	B ▭ Despondent	C ▭ Forlorn	D ▭ Depressed	E ▭ Determined

13	A ▭ Voyage	B ▭ Riddle	C ▭ Trip	D ▭ Outing	E ▭ Expedition

14	A ▭ Fragment	B ▭ Section	C ▭ Byte	D ▭ Bit	E ▭ Scrap

15	A ▭ Prudent	B ▭ Judicious	C ▭ Discreet	D ▭ Pragmatic	E ▭ Unwise

EXERCISE 26: Odd word out

Instructions: Select the word from the each group of words that does not belong to that group.

1	**A** Illusion	**B** Trickery	**C** Tepid	**D** Delusion	**E** Magic

2	**A** Poem	**B** Rhyme	**C** Novel	**D** Ode	**E** Couplet

3	**A** Gold	**B** Copper	**C** Zinc	**D** Steal	**E** Lead

4	**A** Mahogany	**B** Teak	**C** Wood	**D** Walnut	**E** Oak

5	**A** Match	**B** Contest	**C** Competition	**D** Challenge	**E** Victory

6	**A** Poodle	**B** Terrier	**C** Pomeranian	**D** Yak	**E** Borzoi

7	**A** Duke	**B** King	**C** Widower	**D** Enchanter	**E** Sultana

	A	B	C	D	E
8	Lions	Pride	Shoal	Troop	Stud
9	Galaxy	Stars	Skien	Crate	Sheaf
10	Fleet	Cars	Bunch	Sloth	Tribe
11	Gentle	Hairy	Happy	Hungry	Shepherd
12	Porter	Handcuffs	Cobbler	Chauffeur	Glazier
13	Audience	Mob	Rabble	Crowd	Concert
14	Abandon	Forsake	Dessert	Reject	Ditch
15	Cup	Mug	Jug	Spoon	Bowl

EXERCISE 27: Odd word out

Instructions: Select the word from the each group of words that does not belong to that group.

	A	B	C	D	E
1	Bulletin	Forecast	Expect	Predict	Anticipate
2	Gasp	Huff	Puff	Chuff	Pant
3	Legend	Lore	Festive	Myth	Tale
4	Moose	Lapwing	Horse	Hyena	Lynx
5	Glee	Sadness	Grief	Woe	Sorrow
6	Swordfish	Trout	Plaice	Robin	Sole
7	Suppose	Suspect	Guess	Surmise	Solve

Mastering 11+ ™ / English & VR – Book ONE / ashkraft educational

8	**A** ▭ Quaver	**B** ▭ Minim	**C** ▭ Crotchet	**D** ▭ Semiquaver	**E** ▭ Shiver

9	**A** ▭ Oak	**B** ▭ Tin	**C** ▭ Zinc	**D** ▭ Copper	**E** ▭ Gold

10	**A** ▭ Kitten	**B** ▭ Cub	**C** ▭ Kid	**D** ▭ Gosling	**E** ▭ Swan

11	**A** ▭ Marsh	**B** ▭ Swamp	**C** ▭ Bog	**D** ▭ Stream	**E** ▭ Fen

12	**A** ▭ Deject	**B** ▭ Reject	**C** ▭ Scrap	**D** ▭ Discard	**E** ▭ Castoff

13	**A** ▭ Bold	**B** ▭ Italic	**C** ▭ Underline	**D** ▭ Font	**E** ▭ Superscript

14	**A** ▭ Endeavour	**B** ▭ Effort	**C** ▭ Attempt	**D** ▭ Failure	**E** ▭ Try

15	**A** ▭ Sort	**B** ▭ Kind	**C** ▭ Type	**D** ▭ Class	**E** ▭ Bind

EXERCISE 28: Odd word out

Instructions: Select the word from the each group of words that does not belong to that group.

	A	B	C	D	E
1	Fervent	Avid	Ardent	Mediocre	Intense
2	Strike	Assault	Deter	Punch	Pound
3	Succinct	Concise	Brief	Case	Neat
4	Site	Location	Scene	Locality	Sitcom
5	Rubble	Debris	Wreckage	Adage	Remains
6	Mouth	Bay	Bank	Money	Bed
7	Seagull	Redshank	Robin	Stoat	Turkey

8	A ▭ Beet	B ▭ Bacon	C ▭ Bean	D ▭ Broccoli	E ▭ Carrot

9	A ▭ Mars	B ▭ Saturn	C ▭ Pluto	D ▭ Jupiter	E ▭ Earth

10	A ▭ Weasel	B ▭ Yak	C ▭ Zebra	D ▭ Otter	E ▭ Eel

11	A ▭ Chicken	B ▭ Hen	C ▭ Cygnet	D ▭ Calf	E ▭ Fawn

12	A ▭ Pen	B ▭ Fold	C ▭ Web	D ▭ Coop	E ▭ Wasp

13	A ▭ King	B ▭ Man	C ▭ Caravan	D ▭ Soldier	E ▭ Prisoner

14	A ▭ Nice	B ▭ Spinster	C ▭ Lady	D ▭ Sister	E ▭ Uncle

15	A ▭ Roger	B ▭ Yes	C ▭ Wager	D ▭ OK	E ▭ Yeah

ANALOGY

"Victory is the child of preparation and determination"
Sean Hampton

Instructions: Select the best word that completes the word in capitals based on the relationship of the first phrase.

1

Brie is to cheese as SURGEON is to ?

A	B	C	D	E
Medicine	Profession	Student	Mediocre	Doctor

2

Obscurity is to Fame as JOY is to ?

A	B	C	D	E
Thrill	Rapture	Elation	Sorrow	Jewel

3

Copper is to Metal as LIMERICK is to ?

A	B	C	D	E
Poetry	Magician	Wizard	Season	Player

4

Selfish is to Compassion as CHILDISH is to ?

A	B	C	D	E
Maturity	Empathy	Sympathy	Egoistic	Adult

5

Rest is to Relax as IGNITE is to ?

A	B	C	D	E
Burn	Initiate	Kindle	Extinguish	Explode

EXERCISE 30: Analogy

Instructions: Select the best word that completes the word in capitals based on the relationship of the first phrase.

1	**Healthy is to Ill as ELDERLY is to ?**				
	A	**B**	**C**	**D**	**E**
	Youth	Sick	Pension	Retired	Respect

2	**Plane is to Seatbelt as BOAT is to ?**				
	A	**B**	**C**	**D**	**E**
	Raft	Lifejacket	Float	Dinghy	Vessel

3	**Emergency is to Urgent as WIDESPREAD is to ?**				
	A	**B**	**C**	**D**	**E**
	Epidemic	Populate	Common	Disease	Limited

4	**Goal is to Football as Runs is to ?**				
	A	**B**	**C**	**D**	**E**
	Athletic	Olympics	Cricket	Butterfly	Defeat

5	**Mother is to baby as CAT is to ?**				
	A	**B**	**C**	**D**	**E**
	Kitchen	Cub	Pet	Fowl	Kitten

Mastering 11+ ™ / English & VR – Book ONE / ashkraft educational

Instructions: Select the best word that completes the word in capitals based on the relationship of the first phrase.

1 — Athlete is to track as BOXER is to?

A	B	C	D	E
Fight	Punch	Ring	Knockout	Rounds

2 — Pencil is to Lead as PRINTER is to?

A	B	C	D	E
Paper	Cartridge	Tape	Color	Prints

3 — Nobel is to Prize as BOOKER is to?

A	B	C	D	E
Price	Travel	Entertain	Prize	Books

4 — Square is to Area as CUBE is to?

A	B	C	D	E
Perimeter	Volume	Cylinder	Cuboid	Quad

5 — Gigantic is to Huge as MINUTE is to?

A	B	C	D	E
Second	Time	Hour	Multiply	Miniscule

EXERCISE 32: Analogy

Instructions: Select the best word that completes the word in capitals based on the relationship of the first phrase.

1 | **Arachnophobia is to Spider as DENTOPHOBIA is to?**

A	B	C	D	E
☐	☐	☐	☐	☐
Mouth	Dentist	Darkness	Moth	Hospital

2 | **General is to Army as ADMIRAL is to?**

A	B	C	D	E
☐	☐	☐	☐	☐
Navy	Air force	Military	Harbour	Seafront

3 | **Audience is to Concert as CONGREGATION is to?**

A	B	C	D	E
☐	☐	☐	☐	☐
Voyage	Church	Disciples	Election	War

4 | **Paris is to France as EDINBURGH is to?**

A	B	C	D	E
☐	☐	☐	☐	☐
Wales	England	U.K.	Scotland	Ireland

5 | **Japan is to Japanese as AUSTRALIA is to?**

A	B	C	D	E
☐	☐	☐	☐	☐
Australia	Australian	Austrian	English	Asia

 Mastering 11+ ™ / English & VR – Book ONE / ashkraft educational

EXERCISE 33: Analogy

Instructions: Select the best word that completes the word in capitals based on the relationship of the first phrase.

1	**Drink is to Drunk as SLEEP is to?**				
	A ▭ Sleep	▭ Asleep	**C** ▭ Dream	**D** ▭ Slept	**E** ▭ Swept

2	**Profit is to Loss as ASSET is to?**				
	A ▭ Liability	**B** ▭ Loan	**C** ▭ Debt	**D** ▭ Negate	**E** ▭ Account

3	**Mobile is to Immobile as REACTIVE is to?**				
	A ▭ Active	**B** ▭ Proactive	**C** ▭ Inactive	**D** ▭ Action	**E** ▭ Reaction

4	**Paris is to France as London is to?**				
	A ▭ U.K.	**B** ▭ Scotland	**C** ▭ Ireland	**D** ▭ Europe	**E** ▭ England

5	**Lock is to Unlock as MEND is to?**				
	A ▭ Fix	**B** ▭ Break	**C** ▭ Repair	**D** ▭ Mess	**E** ▭ Mean

EXERCISE 34: Analogy

Instructions: Select the best word that completes the word in capitals based on the relationship of the first phrase.

1 **Rule is to Govern as DOWNFALL is to?**

A	B	C	D	E
Downsize	Ruin	Raise	Assist	Democracy

2 **Rich is to Fertile as POOR is to?**

A	B	C	D	E
Meagre	Noble	Upright	Virtuous	Just

3 **Brave is to Craven as ANGRY is to?**

A	B	C	D	E
Furious	Calm	Tactical	Sure	Red

4 **Ignore is to Overlook as NOTICE is to?**

A	B	C	D	E
Observe	Inform	Indicate	Serve	Obsolve

5 **Racquet is to Tennis as CLUB is to?**

A	B	C	D	E
Group	Society	Drive	Range	Golf

Mastering 11+ ™ / English & VR – Book ONE / ashkraft educational

EXERCISE 35: Analogy

Instructions: Select the best word that completes the word in capitals based on the relationship of the first phrase.

1 | **Daylight is to Dawn as Nightfall is to ?**

A	B	C	D	E
Dawn	Darkness	Dream	Dusk	Tide

2 | **Stout is Hefty as TIMID is to ?**

A	B	C	D	E
Shy	Fear	Clever	Interior	Success

3 | **Rage is to Fume as CHARM is to ?**

A	B	C	D	E
Cajole	Frenzy	Trend	Mania	Anger

4 | **Comedy is to Tragedy as LAUGH is to?**

A	B	C	D	E
Scare	Cry	Gulp	Plum	Giggle

5 | **Undo is to Fasten as NERVE is to?**

A	B	C	D	E
Guts	Slow	Cowardice	Impudent	Cheeky

ANSWERS

"A winning effort begins with preparation"
Joe Gibbs

ANSWERS:

EXERCISE 1 Matching Words		EXERCISE 2 Matching Words		EXERCISE 3 Matching Words		EXERCISE 4 Matching Words		EXERCISE 5 Matching Words	
1	C	1	C	1	C	1	B	1	D
2	B	2	B	2	E	2	A	2	E
3	B	3	A	3	B	3	A	3	A
4	A	4	C	4	B	4	E	4	B
5	D	5	A	5	B	5	A	5	A
6	A	6	B	6	C	6	A	6	A
7	D	7	A	7	A	7	A	7	A
8	A	8	A	8	B	8	C	8	C
9	E	9	A	9	E	9	E	9	A
10	A	10	A	10	A	10	A	10	C
11	C	11	E	11	D	11	A	11	A
12	A	12	D	12	B	12	A	12	B
13	B	13	C	13	C	13	A	13	A
14	B	14	B	14	B	14	D	14	D
15	A	15	A	15	A	15	E	15	A

ANSWERS:

EXERCISE 6 Matching Words		EXERCISE 7 Matching Words		EXERCISE 8 Opposite Words		EXERCISE 9 Opposite Words		EXERCISE 10 Opposite Words	
1	B	1	C	1	A	1	E	1	E
2	A	2	B	2	B	2	B	2	A
3	B	3	B	3	D	3	D	3	B
4	A	4	A	4	B	4	E	4	C
5	B	5	C	5	D	5	E	5	D
6	A	6	A	6	B	6	B	6	B
7	B	7	A	7	A	7	A	7	C
8	C	8	D	8	C	8	C	8	D
9	D	9	B	9	C	9	D	9	D
10	B	10	A	10	A	10	E	10	E
11	D	11	C	11	C	11	D	11	E
12	A	12	A	12	C	12	E	12	E
13	A	13	B	13	A	13	A	13	D
14	A	14	B	14	D	14	C	14	D
15	B	15	A	15	A	15	E	15	D

ANSWERS:

EXERCISE 11 Opposite Words		EXERCISE 12 Opposite Words		EXERCISE 13 Opposite Words		EXERCISE 14 Opposite Words		EXERCISE 15 Complete the word	
1	A	1	E	1	C	1	A	1	RI
2	A	2	C	2	A	2	A	2	PP
3	A	3	C	3	C	3	A	3	AC
4	C	4	C	4	A	4	C	4	OO
5	C	5	C	5	A	5	C	5	CA
6	D	6	A	6	C	6	B	6	OM
7	A	7	A	7	C	7	E	7	ND
8	C	8	A	8	D	8	C	8	OU
9	D	9	C	9	A	9	E	9	SY
10	D	10	A	10	D	10	C	10	LE
11	D	11	A	11	C	11	A	11	ON
12	A	12	E	12	D	12	A	12	AK
13	E	13	D	13	C	13	B	13	IE
14	E	14	B	14	D	14	C	14	IL
15	E	15	C	15	C	15	B	15	AV

ANSWERS:

EXERCISE 16 Complete the word		EXERCISE 17 Complete the word		EXERCISE 18 Complete the word		EXERCISE 19 Complete the word		EXERCISE 20 Complete the word	
1	LE	1	AK	1	IG	1	VE	1	LL
2	RE	2	OA	2	OW	2	IE	2	ZE
3	AE	3	OT	3	ME	3	LP	3	ST
4	ID	4	EE	4	EE	4	PR	4	AL
5	NT	5	LY	5	MT	5	RE	5	OK
6	GT	6	DR	6	RD	6	CE	6	LS
7	DE	7	LO	7	LK	7	IE	7	PE
8	FE	8	VB	8	TL	8	IS	8	CT
9	IH	9	NI	9	AR	9	GE	9	MK
10	AN	10	SL	10	SO	10	US	10	LE
11	RA	11	GG	11	IE	11	OR	11	IC
12	IE	12	OL	12	NE	12	CR	12	FS
13	KE	13	OE	13	AC	13	EN	13	HE
14	IL	14	IE	14	NE	14	UT	14	OF
15	RE	15	OO	15	AY	15	AE	15	LR

ANSWERS:

EXERCISE 21 Complete the word		EXERCISE 22 Odd word		EXERCISE 23 Odd word		EXERCISE 24 Odd word		EXERCISE 25 Odd word	
1	NC	1	D	1	A	1	E	1	C
2	AW	2	D	2	B	2	B	2	C
3	OR	3	C	3	D	3	D	3	E
4	RS	4	E	4	C	4	E	4	C
5	ER	5	C	5	D	5	B	5	B
6	RU	6	D	6	B	6	D	6	B
7	CK	7	D	7	D	7	E	7	D
8	LM	8	B	8	D	8	D	8	A
9	TE	9	E	9	C	9	E	9	B
10	OT	10	E	10	A	10	C	10	E
11	ER	11	C	11	E	11	A	11	D
12	QU	12	A	12	D	12	C	12	E
13	GE	13	E	13	C	13	E	13	B
14	WE	14	E	14	B	14	D	14	C
15	EE	15	A	15	C	15	D	15	E

ANSWERS:

EXERCISE 26 Odd word		EXERCISE 27 Odd word		EXERCISE 28 Odd word		EXERCISE 29 Analogy		EXERCISE 30 Analogy	
1	C	1	A	1	D	1	E	1	A
2	C	2	D	2	C	2	D	2	B
3	D	3	C	3	D	3	A	3	A
4	C	4	B	4	E	4	A	4	C
5	E	5	A	5	D	5	B	5	E
6	D	6	D	6	D				
7	E	7	B	7	D				
8	A	8	E	8	B				
9	B	9	A	9	C				
10	B	10	E	10	D				
11	E	11	D	11	B				
12	B	12	A	12	E				
13	E	13	D	13	C				
14	C	14	D	14	E				
15	D	15	E	15	C				

ANSWERS:

EXERCISE 31 Analogy		EXERCISE 32 Analogy		EXERCISE 33 Analogy		EXERCISE 34 Analogy		EXERCISE 35 Analogy	
1	C	1	B	1	D	1	B	1	D
2	B	2	A	2	A	2	A	2	A
3	D	3	B	3	B	3	B	3	A
4	B	4	D	4	E	4	A	4	B
5	E	5	B	5	B	5	E	5	A

Other books in the **Mastering 11+** series:

- ➢ English & Verbal Reasoning – Practice Book 2
- ➢ English & Verbal Reasoning – Practice Book 3

- ➢ Cloze Tests – Practice Book 1
- ➢ Cloze Tests – Practice Book 2
- ➢ Cloze Tests – Practice Book 3

- ➢ Maths – Practice Book 1
- ➢ Maths – Practice Book 2
- ➢ Maths – Practice Book 3

- ➢ Comprehension – Multiple Choice Exercise Book 1
- ➢ Comprehension – Multiple Choice Exercise Book 2
- ➢ Comprehension – Multiple Choice Exercise Book 3

- ➢ CEM Practice Papers – Pack 1
- ➢ CEM Practice Papers – Pack 2
- ➢ CEM Practice Papers – Pack 3
- ➢ CEM Practice Papers – Pack 4

All queries to **enquiry@mastering11plus.com**

Printed in Great Britain
by Amazon.co.uk, Ltd.,
Marston Gate.